Portrait of Fear

A play

Edward Taylor

Samuel French — London
New York - Toronto - Hollywood

PORTRAIT OF FEAR

First presented, with the title *The Face of Fear*, at the Mill
Theatre, Sonning-on-Thames, on 25th February 2004,
with the following cast:

Sir Christopher Camberston	Nick Waring
Selena Harris	Rae Baker
Peter Sims	Michael Cheyney
Terri Coleman	Abi Harris
Joe	Ryan Romain

Directed by Sally Hughes

CHARACTERS

Sir Christopher (Kit) Camberston, owner of Renfield
  House, late 20s
Selena Harris, TV presenter, late 20s
Peter Sims, Selena's husband, TV producer, late 20s
Terri Coleman, TV researcher, mid-twenties
Joe, TV technician, young

SYNOPSIS OF SCENES

The action of the play takes place in the Tower Room of
Renfield House (ancestral home of the Camberston family)

ACT I

SCENE 1   An afternoon in November
SCENE 2   Five minutes later

ACT II

SCENE 1   Fifteen minutes later
SCENE 2   Two minutes later

Time — the present

Other plays by Edward Taylor published by Samuel French Ltd

Murder by Misadventure
A Rise in the Market
Pardon Me, Prime Minister (with John Graham)

ACT I

SCENE 1

The Tower Room at Renfield House. An afternoon in winter

There are long windows at the rear of the room leading on to a stone balcony; floor-length curtains hang at the windows. The walls are panelled and there is a single door. The room has, for many years, been used only for storage; the furniture, which includes a piano, chairs and a chaise-longue, is covered by dust sheets, as are the pictures on the walls. One of the pictures, c of the rear wall, has a shelf beneath it upon which stands a small vase containing drooping flowers. Various other objects — including two Indian clubs — and boxes are lying around

When the CURTAIN *rises the room's floor-length curtains are closed but slightly parted, letting in some grey, wintry light. The daylight outside fades to darkness as the scene proceeds*

After a moment we hear the piano playing softly and then, faintly, the sound of a woman sobbing. These sounds fade and there comes another noise: a fluttering and soft thumping, as of a trapped bird trying to escape through a closed window. The noise ceases. There's a short silence

We hear the sound of a large old key, reluctantly turning in a large old lock, and the door creaks open

Sir Christopher "Kit" Camberston enters, walking with the aid of a silver-knobbed stick. He shows in Selena Harris, who is wearing a distinctive baseball-style jacket with "Crescent TV" embossed on the back, and carrying a handbag

During the following dialogue Kit leaves the door open, puts on an overhead light and draws back the curtains to reveal an angry winter sky. He then removes dust sheets from a few chairs and the chaise-longue. When the first chair is uncovered, Selena removes the jacket and puts it on the seat

Kit Here we are. (*He coughs*) Sorry about the dust. I'm afraid the servants won't come in here any more.
Selena Sounds promising.
Kit Depends on your point of view. Personally, I'd rather have a usable music room than a notorious chamber of horrors.

Selena At least your ghosts have brought us together again. Thank you, Kit, for letting us come here. It shows a very generous spirit.

Kit It's the least one can do for an old friend. Besides, I'm quite glad of the fee. The Camberston coffers are sounding a bit hollow at present.

Selena I'm glad we're still friends. There are no ill feelings then?

Kit No point in ill feelings, is there? You had to do what was best for you.

Selena Best for both of us, I think.

Kit How have things worked out? I'm afraid I don't watch much telly, but I saw you once or twice on that late night magazine thing.

Selena "Witching Hour"? Yes, I did that for a couple of years. Then I fronted the travel programme. Eventually, I got tired of having producers tell me what to do, and I decided I wanted to be my own boss.

Kit Ah. I remember that attitude from college. You left Dr Moore rather shaken, I think.

Selena You mean, because *I* told *him* what essays I should write?

Kit I was thinking more of when you told him what thesis he should write. So, did you and Peter get married? He didn't say when he called. Or are you just "partners", in the modern manner?

Selena Both. Yes, we did get married, just after university. I told you we were going to.

Kit You did. But then you once told people that about me.

Selena Well, circumstances were rather different, weren't they?

Kit They certainly were.

Selena Perhaps we shouldn't be talking about that now. But, just to answer your question, we are married. And we're business partners as well.

Kit Cosy.

Selena Cosy. And practical. While I was under contract to the Beeb, Peter was writing and directing, learning the ropes. When I chose to go freelance, we set up our own production company. And here we are.

Kit Is "Paranormal" your first project?

Selena Oh no. We did "Exploring Britain" two years ago, plus a couple of regional chat shows. Last year we had a cookery programme on the network, and we made a pop-science series that hasn't gone out yet. But "Paranormal" will be the big one.

Kit I hope so. It's a good idea. I'm surprised no-one's done it before.

Selena Not in quite the way we're doing it. Each week, an in-depth study of a famous haunted house, using modern technology. With luck, we might catch a ghost on screen.

Kit And you chose to start here.

Selena Well, Borley Rectory burned down, and Anfield Manor didn't want to know us — it seems they're ashamed of their ghost, 'cos he's a bit common. Renfield House is the obvious place. Most people have heard of it. And it helps to be in with the management.

Kit I hope our ghosts don't let you down. (*Looking around*) I'm afraid there's not much light in here. Will this be enough for you?

Selena Oh no, we need very bright lights. But don't worry, we bring our own. The crew will be unloading them now.

Kit Only one power point, I'm afraid. And I'm not sure I trust that.

Selena No problem. Peter worked it all out when he did his recce. We travel with our own generator.

Peter enters through the open door. He's a down-to-earth, practical chap, in sweater and jeans. He is carrying some equipment, including a tall light stand and lamp. He has a mobile phone in a holder on his belt

Ah. And Peter Sims said "Let there be light!"

Kit Come in, Peter.

Peter (*to Kit*) Hi. (*To Selena*) We took some exteriors. Just caught the light.

Selena You got some good shots?

Peter Right. This place is fantastic! No matter what angle you take it from, it's hideous!

Kit Thanks.

Peter No offence, it's what we want. All right if we start setting up in here now?

Kit Of course. Make yourself at home. Sorry there's no-one to help carry your gear.

Peter That's OK, there's three of us. (*Indicating Selena; light-heartedly*) Not our star, of course. Insurance company rules.

During the following Peter busies himself planning the layout and setting up

Selena You don't run this place all on your own, Kit?

Kit Almost. My only regular staff are the Websters. Mrs is the cook-housekeeper, he's the handyman-chauffeur. Then there's a girl who comes in once a week to clean.

Peter You're still not allowed to drive?

Kit The ban ended last year. But I prefer not to.

Peter I can understand that.

Kit Anyway, no Websters today, I'm afraid. They asked for the day off. They heartily disapprove of what you're doing.

Selena Really?

Kit Mrs Webster was the last to have a bad experience here.

Selena When was that?

Kit Last year. She was bringing some boxes in and felt a sudden chill. Then a heavy oak hat-stand toppled over for no apparent reason. Missed her by inches. Since then, the room's been locked up again.

Peter (*puzzled*) Exactly how long ago was that?

Kit It was summer, I remember. So it must have been at least fourteen months ago.

Peter No-one's been in here for fourteen months?

Kit Apart from you, on your first visit.

Peter So how do you explain these flowers? (*He indicates the vase of drooping flowers* UC)

Kit Good Lord! Well, I can't explain them. I think Mrs Webster used to put flowers in here years ago. She felt sorry for Philomel. But, as I said, nowadays she won't come near the place. (*He moves over to inspect the flowers*) Mind you, they're pretty dead.

Peter But not fourteen months dead. They're not dried up. And look, there's still some water in the vase.

Kit Odd. Of course, this room is very airless. Perhaps it's like preserving things in a sealed box.

This speculation is interrupted by the arrival of Terri Coleman through the open door. She's in her mid-twenties, attractive but intense and eccentric. She, too, brings equipment — some in a rucksack on her back, some loose, including a freestanding thermometer

Peter moves over and takes some of the things from her during the following

Peter Ah, Terri. Christopher, you met Terri when we came last month.

Kit Of course. Good to see you again, Miss ... er ...

Terri Just call me Terri. God, there's a tension in this place you could cut with a knife. We're really going to get something here!

Selena Terri's our researcher and psychic consultant. She's also a gifted medium, which is rather convenient for this job.

Kit Indeed. And what on earth is that device?

Terri It's an electronic thermometer. It reacts to psychic phenomena.

Kit You mean, you can tell when there's a ghost about?

Terri Sometimes. When supernatural forces are active, there's often a drop in temperature.

Kit Well, that's happened here often enough. Now you said you felt tension in this room. Is that showing up on the thermometer?

Terri peers at the thermometer

Terri No. Latent forces won't do it. There has to be activity. Psychic forces can also cause a change in the magnetic field. We have a magnetometer to spot that.

Kit Ah. Well, perhaps you could give me an idea of your schedule for the evening. I'd like to help in any way I can.

Peter We'll be a while yet setting up, and then we'll take a break. It's been a long drive from London. After that, we'll get down to serious business.

Kit The séance?

Peter Exactly. Terri will see if we can tempt your ghosts out of the woodwork.

Selena But first I'll interview you, Kit, about the house and its history.

Kit Hm. That's more frightening than the ghosts. Do I have to do it?

Peter (*lightly*) 'Fraid so. It's in the contract we signed.

Selena (*lightly*) Always read the small print, especially when dealing with rogues and vagabonds from TV.

Kit I'll remember that.

During the following, Selena and Kit find comfortable perches. Peter and Terri busy themselves setting up equipment, but they pay attention and break off their work when appropriate

Selena Actually, Kit, if you could give us a briefing while we're setting up, it would save a lot of time later.

Kit A briefing?

Selena Tell us all you can about the ghosts of Renfield House. We've done our research, of course, but I doubt we've got the full picture. Rehearse the story before you go on camera.

Kit Well, yes, that might help, I suppose. I'd better start by saying that, with one possible exception, no-one's seen an actual ghost here. I mean, there's no record of figures in sheets walking through walls with their heads underneath their arms.

Terri We weren't expecting pantomime ghosts, Sir Christopher. It's psychic phenomena we're after.

Kit Well, there's been plenty of that — unexplained noises, music, poltergeist activity. Sudden falls in temperature, plus that curious tension you sensed just now, Miss ... er ...

Terri Terri.

Selena You said there might be an exception, someone who actually saw something.

Kit Possibly. Back in the 1920s. As a young man, my great-grandfather was in with a rather wild bunch. Sort of latter-day Hellfire Club. Too much money and not enough sense. Fast cars — drink — possibly drugs. Bloody idiots. And, before you say anything, Peter, yes, it's in the genes.

Peter I wouldn't say a word.

Kit Good. Well, one of his cronies — who rejoiced in the name of Fruity French — stayed locked in this room all night for a bet. At least, he tried to stay all night, but he didn't quite make it.

Selena How so?

Kit About three in the morning he started screaming the place down. Before anyone could get here and unlock the door, he'd gone out over the balcony and broken his neck.

Peter Oh dear. Fractured French.

Kit Quite. He was semi-conscious when they found him, babbling about someone in white, with a knife. And his hair had gone white, to match. He died in hospital the next day.

Selena Wow! Thank you for that, Kit. We could re-enact that as an opener for the programme! What d'you think, Peter?

Peter Great.

Kit Doesn't prove anything, of course. The poor fool could have been out of his mind with drink, or worse. Then again, the gang could have been playing tricks on him. Or even something nastier.

Peter Nastier?

Kit There were rumours that Fruity French had been seeing rather too much of my great-grandmother.

Selena Take us back to the original tragedy, Kit. The business that started it all. The story of Philomel.

Kit I expect you know it. The tale's been told a few times.

Selena I'd like to hear it from you, Kit. As you'll do it on the programme.

Kit All right. 1852. My ancestor Richard Camberston, the Sixth Baronet. He was a great traveller and trader, much involved with West Indian sugar. He had skirmishes with pirates in the Caribbean, in one of which he was shot in the leg. He walked with a limp ever since.

Terri Just like you!

Kit Ah, you noticed. Yes, just like me. He was a widower for years; he married his second wife late in life, and brought her to live here in Renfield House.

Terri And this was Philomel?

Kit This was Philomel. That's her picture on the wall over there. (*He moves across and takes the dust sheet from the picture* c *of the rear wall*)

The picture is revealed to be the portrait of a beautiful young woman, not dissimilar to Selena. The onlookers express admiration

Peter Beautiful. We can use that as a background to the titles.

Kit Philomel was regarded as a great beauty. Also very musical. She spent hours in here, playing that piano.

Peter Portrait and piano music behind captions. Fantastic.

Kit She loved horses. And it seems one of the grooms took a fancy to her. In fact, he became obsessed by Philomel. And he actually began to fantasize that she returned his feelings. One day, when he thought Richard was out, this chap — Paul Hunte, his name was — came in here and started to force his attentions upon her. And when she resisted he cut her throat with a saddle knife.

Peter Nasty.

Kit In fact, Richard was only in the orchard, shooting pigeons. He heard her screams and came rushing up here.

Terri In spite of his limp.

Kit Men with limps can be quite active, young woman. Richard was in time to shoot Hunte dead. But not in time to save his wife.

Selena Poor Philomel.

Kit And poor Richard. He was absolved at the inquest, of course. But he was heartbroken. Ironic that the groom, Hunte, was an orphan boy he'd rescued on his travels.

Selena And Richard came to a sad end, didn't he?

Kit I suppose it was sad. Actually, after losing Philomel, I don't think he cared if he lived or died. He started travelling again, and was drowned two years later.

Terri Drowned?

Kit His ship, the *Lotus*, sank off Jamaica.

Peter When did the haunting start?

Kit It's not clear. Richard locked this room after the tragedy, and it remained so for years. Richard's heir was Nicholas, his son by his first wife. Nicholas respected his father's wishes and kept the room locked. But his son, Henry, thought it was all nonsense, and brought the room back into use as a music room.

Selena Wasn't Henry's boy the first to experience something strange?

Kit It seems so. In a letter to a friend, he said the room terrified him. He had musical talent, and played well everywhere else. But here in the music room he couldn't play a note. He said his fingers felt frozen.

Selena Was there something about a vase?

Kit He said he saw a vase of flowers fly through the air and smash against a wall. Of course, no-one believed him. They all thought he'd broken the vase and was covering up.

Terri If the boy was musical, that's what got the spirits going.

Kit Probably.

Terri Ghosts can lie dormant for years, until someone comes along with the right vibes. Someone they can relate to.

Kit I'm sure. After that, it's a succession of scared servants leaving, and people hearing odd noises — music and some sort of sobbing, apparently.

Selena They heard them when they were outside the room?

Kit Or thought they did. Whenever anyone came in to check, there was silence. Oh, and there's been another curious thing.

Selena Yes?

Kit It appears Philomel adored the scent of violets. And, at times of odd activity here — the music, the poltergeists, and so on — people have sometimes said they smelled violets. My great-grandfather reported it the night French died.

Selena What about other incidents over the years?

Kit My great-grandfather got very keen and did some research into family letters and diaries. He produced a catalogue of mysterious goings on, with lots of details and dates. He was able to provide a whole chapter for A.P. Lyall's "Ghosts of Great Britain."

Selena And is all that in your library now?

Kit Oh yes. Just downstairs.

Selena Could I go and study it?

Kit By all means. I'll come down and show you.

Terri One other request, Sir Christopher.

Kit Yes?

Terri Is there any private possession of Philomel's left in the house? Something small and personal I could borrow for the séance?

Kit There's some jewellery that's been passed down the female side of the family. It may be in my late mother's dressing table. I'll have a look.

Joe comes in through the open door. He is a robust, cheerful, young extrovert, and brings more equipment, including another lamp stand and lamp

Peter Come in, Joe. What kept you?

Joe Looking at the map, boss. Working on a better way home. We needn't have come through Southbury at all.

Peter Really? Well, just remember you're here as techie, not travel guide. Christopher, this is Joe, our engineer.

Joe Hi.

Kit How d'you do. Welcome to Renfield House.

Selena Joe's working with us for the first time. He's depping for our regular man, who's got a broken ankle.

Kit Poor chap.

Peter He came here on our recce, if you remember. Got very interested, and started studying poltergeists on the Internet. Last week his computer fell on his foot. Joe, let's get the lights set, and link up the generator.

Joe Yeah, OK. Only I don't fancy running the cables up that twisty staircase.

Peter I thought about that. (*Moving to the balcony doors*) Christopher — is there any access to the roof from this balcony?

Kit joins Peter, opens one of the balcony doors, and points

Kit Yes. There's an iron ladder at the end.

Peter Good. Would you mind if we put the generator up above and dropped the cables down?

Kit Not at all. Do whatever suits you.

Peter Right. Joe, let's start getting wired up.

Joe Sure. We're going to be filming ghosts, right?

Selena We hope so. If Terri can conjure them up.

Peter She'd better or we don't have a programme.

Joe I reckon ghosts'll need a whole lot of light. One question, boss — when do we get a break?

Peter About thirty minutes. I'd like to see the lights working first.

Joe I'm starving. I could eat a horse.

Peter In the local eaterie, you probably will. Where's the nearest pub, Christopher?

Kit The *Pear Tree*, down in the village. But you won't need to go out. I had Mrs Webster set up a cold buffet in the dining-room before she left.

Selena That's very kind of you, Kit.

Kit And I have a rather good claret I'd like you to try.

Peter Oh. (*Grudgingly*) Well ... Very kind, as Selena said. But I think we all need a hot meal after that journey. And I'm more of a draught beer man than a claret swiller.

Joe Me too. Have they got a good bitter down the *Pear Tree*?

Kit I'm afraid I wouldn't know. I thought smoked salmon and cold pheasant would be enough for you.

Peter The pub's part of our routine, Christopher. So I'm afraid the answer is thanks, but no thanks.

Selena We've got a couple of rough diamonds here, I'm afraid, Kit. We'd better let them go. Personally, I shall be delighted to join you for the buffet.

Peter No, Selena. You know we've got things to discuss. We said all along we'd work them out at the pub. I'm directing this show. I want you there.

Kit Good Lord! Do you have to take that from him, Selena?

Selena 'Fraid so. When you're making a programme, the director calls the shots.

Kit So be it. I'm sorry your manners haven't improved since college, Peter. But I suppose television is scarcely the right environment to develop graceful behaviour.

Peter There's no need to be bloody insulting! We're a team, right? And I want my whole crew together for a team talk, right? Nitty gritty. I don't want to ponce around eating prawns-in-aspic and making polite conversation!

Kit I'm sure that's something you'd never do. However, we have a professional contract, so I'll leave you to carry it out. Selena, I'll show you the library, if you're ready.

Selena Thank you. Is there paper for making notes?

Kit Plenty. Oh, and I'll try to find something of Philomel's for you, Miss …
    er … Terri.

Kit and Selena exit

*Peter, Joe and Terri resume their setting-up. During the following, Joe sets
at least one lamp in place on a high tripod; a screwdriver is left beneath it*

Joe I reckon we've upset the duke.

Peter That's not difficult. Fifteen generations of chinless wonders, who've
    always got their own way. It's not surprising if the end of the line's a bit
    touchy.

Terri I think he's weird. When we came down for that business chat, he gave
    me the creeps.

Joe Can't see how he'd give you the creeps. He's just a posh git, isn't he?
    Too soft to frighten anyone.

Terri You think that, and then you catch him looking at you as if he'd like
    to chain you up in a dungeon and do unspeakable things.

Joe (*enthusiastically*) Cor! Wish he'd throw a party!

Terri And another thing. Last time we were here, he didn't know what he
    was doing half the time.

Joe You're joking!

Peter It's true, I'm afraid. Camberston has these blackouts. Zonks out for ten
    minutes and can't remember what happened.

Joe Blimey! You gotta feel sorry for him then.

Peter No, you haven't. He brought it on himself. You heard him talk about
    his great-grandfather being a hellraiser. Well, the old timer had nothing on
    this pratt. Drink — drugs — and I don't just mean pot. He lived like a
    lunatic, and wrecked his health.

Joe You were at college with him, boss?

Peter I was, yes, and Selena too. That's where we all met. When I was
    swotting for exams, the noise from Camberston's room kept me awake all
    night. Of course, he wasn't bothered about work, being due to cop the
    family fortune. Anyone like me, who had to work to get on, he heartily
    despised.

Terri Is it true he and Selena were an item?

Peter Yes, but don't hold it against her. He could be quite impressive when
    you first met him. It was a while before she found he was into boozing and
    snorting. Then she thought she could reform him.

Terri And did she? Doesn't seem like he's too wild now. More just creepy,
    like I said.

Peter As far as we know. But no, it needed more than a good woman to bring
    Camberston round. It took a bloody car smash.

Terri A car smash?

Peter On the way home from a party, Camberston drove his Lotus into a tree. He was sloshed out of his mind, of course.

Terri *Lotus*! That was the ship that drowned his ancestor!

Peter Interesting.

Joe Is that how he got that limp?

Peter Yes. He got away with a broken leg. His passenger wasn't so lucky. She was killed.

Terri My God! You never told me any of this before!

Peter We don't broadcast these things, Selena was fond of him. I only speak out when his arrogance gets too much for me.

Joe Was he done for drunken driving?

Peter Yes. He was lucky not to get done for manslaughter. I think there were some strings pulled in high places. He just got six months in jail and a long ban.

Terri Was that when Selena broke the engagement?

Peter Yes. She was entitled to. She'd been trying to straighten him out for a year. The last straw was the girl in the car — a local tart he'd promised not to see any more.

Terri I wonder if Sir Richard was a rake in 1852, and Philomel tried to straighten him out.

Peter Well, if anyone can tell us, Terri, it'll be you. (*He finishes a task*) See if you can finish the connections, Joe, and get the other lamp up. I'll go down and get the generator.

Joe OK, boss. (*He continues his work, which includes moving the piano slightly*)

Terri takes a notepad from her rucksack and makes notes in it

Joe Done all this before, have you, Terri?

Terri Yes and no. I've made plenty of programmes with Crescent TV. And I've done psychic research as a hobby. This is the first time I've combined the two. Actually, "Paranormal" is my idea — though I don't think you'd get Peter or Selena to say so.

Joe I bet. Shame you have to work backstage. A chick as cool as you should be swanning about on camera, like Selena.

Terri Forget it. I like the creative side — thinking up ideas, researching, finding out the facts.

Joe With a figure like yours, you could be a model.

Terri Thanks, but I've no ambition to be an animated clothes horse.

Joe You could always take the clothes off, if you wanted.

Terri In your dreams, sunshine. You do know, don't you, that we need the recording gear so finely tuned it'll hear a pin drop?

Joe No problem. When I've done, it'll pick up the sound of someone changing their mind.

Terri It had better.

Joe You got a boyfriend, Terri?

Terri That's a bit personal, isn't it?

Joe Only Saturday night I'm going to a party. Thought you might like to come.

Terri Tell me about it tomorrow. Let's get the job done first. Do you feel cold?

Joe Yeah. Well, it's dark now, isn't it? We should feel cold in this old ruin.

Terri But it happened suddenly. When you moved the piano. (*She peers at the thermometer*) Look, the thermo's down!

Joe It's a November night, love. It would be down. Where's my screwdriver? I left it here.

Terri I can smell violets!

Joe (*amused*) You started calling up your ghosts already?

Terri They don't need calling up, they're here! My God, this room's explosive!

Joe Look, you want to lark about with spooks, you go ahead. But don't start moving my gear! Where's my bleeding screwdriver? It was here! (*He looks around and sees the screwdriver a small distance away, close to the lamp stand*)

The overhead light flickers during the following

Gawd! How did it get over there, if you didn't move it? Your spooks, I suppose!

Terri Right! A poltergeist!

Joe That's a new one — ghosts wanting a screw! (*Reacting to the flickering lights*) Bloody hell, now the overhead's going! ... (*He moves towards the screwdriver*)

Terri (*in a panic*) No, Joe, don't go over there! It's a trap!

But Joe continues towards the screwdriver and the lamp stand. As he does so, all the lights snap to Black-out

The CURTAIN *falls*

As it does so, we hear an enormous crash, and a cry of pain from Joe

The same. Five minutes later

The overhead light is on again. The lamp from the high stand lies on the floor, where it fell after it hit Joe

Joe sits in a chair, rubbing a painful shoulder; Terri is helping him

Joe Bloody thing! Nearly bust my shoulder!

Terri Well, it's definitely not broken.

Joe Don't stop, I'm enjoying it.

Terri Be grateful it wasn't worse. That was meant to smash your head.

Joe (*derisively*) What d'you mean, meant to? You think someone pushed it with an invisible hand?

Terri Someone or something. Having moved the screwdriver first, to get you lined up.

Joe Cobblers! It toppled over on the uneven surface, that's all. This floor's as worn as a tart's staircase.

Terri Don't be flippant, Joe. There are spirits active in this room. Strong spirits.

Joe Well, there are stronger spirits down the pub. The sooner we get there, the better.

Selena enters, carrying a notebook

Selena Terri, I've got some exciting stuff ... Hallo, what's happening here?

Terri Poltergeist activity. The big lamp came down on Joe.

Selena I heard a crash like World War Three. I thought someone had dropped the generator.

Joe Don't worry, it's nothing. Forget poltergeists. The lamp tipped over on the bumpy floor.

Terri Joe's a sceptic. Or, to put it another way, he's thick. This place is teeming with hostile forces.

Selena It's certainly very tense.

Terri We need the séance as soon as possible. Try and release these tortured spirits. There's turbulence here that's almost unbearable.

Joe There's turbulence in my gut that *is* unbearable! I want my supper! (*He gets up and resumes his work on the equipment*)

Kit enters

Kit What was the bang I heard? Is everyone all right?

Selena Yes, but the lamp went over and gave Joe a knock. Terri believes it was psychic activity.

Kit Like Mrs Webster's hat-stand. Are you hurt, young man?

Joe No. I keep telling them, it's nothing to do with psychic. It went over 'cos your floor's dodgy.

Kit Along with the walls and ceiling. The whole place is only held together by the Death Watch Beetles holding hands. (*He produces a locket*) I have a locket of Philomel's for you, Miss ... er ... Terri. I hope it's the sort of thing you wanted.

Terri Sounds great. (*She moves across and takes the locket from Kit*) Mm, it's lovely!

Kit It is rather, isn't it? I don't know anything about its history. But it was definitely Philomel's. Or so my mother told me.

Terri Thanks. I can really work on this.

Selena I found some interesting stuff in the library, Kit. I didn't realize Renfield House featured in the Civil War.

Kit Only marginally. The Camberstons were Royalists, of course. My ancestor used the house as a recruiting centre for the king's army. One of the volunteers was found to be a spy, and was hanged.

Joe They didn't mess about in them days, did they?

Terri When was Renfield House actually built?

Kit At the start of the seventeenth century.

Terri That's what it says in my notes. But, looking round when we got here, it struck me as older. Some of those outside walls seem medieval. And that hole in the yard looks like an oubliette.

Kit Bright girl. Yes, Renfield House was built on the ruins of a ninth-century Saxon castle, and some of the original walls were retained.

Terri Ninth century! Wow!

Kit Some old masonry still survives. And, of course, the oubliette is genuine.

Joe What's an oubliette?

Kit Well, basically, it's a deep hole, a bit like a well. You could chuck anyone you didn't much like down there, and be pretty sure you wouldn't see them again.

Joe Charming!

Kit The lord of the castle might drop his enemies in the oubliette if he was a bit religious, and didn't want their blood on his hands. Then no-one could say he'd killed them, but they wouldn't give him any more trouble.

Selena Ideal for double glazing salesmen.

Kit Once you were down there you were forgotten. The name comes from the French *oublier* — to forget.

Joe Oh yeah. I forgot.

Peter storms in, on the warpath, and marches up to Kit

During the ensuing quarrel, Terri and Joe get on with various tasks and try to fade into the woodwork. One spotlight is set up pointing directly at the portrait C

Peter My God, Camberston, you really don't want us to go to the pub, do you? But I didn't think you'd go to those lengths!

Kit What on earth are you talking about?

Peter You know damned well what I'm talking about! You sabotaged the bloody van, didn't you?

Kit Sabotaged the van?

Selena Peter, what is all this? What's happened?

Peter I went back to the van just now, and all the tyres are flat! Someone's let them down! And it's not difficult to guess who did it!

Kit Good God! You think I let the tyres down on your van? That's absurd!

Selena Don't be ridiculous, Peter. Kit wouldn't go around letting down people's tyres!

Peter Wouldn't he? What about our first year in college? When he and his chums took the saddles off all the bikes in the bike shed and burned them? Or the time they put Superglue in the locks? Practical jokes, it's called. Very funny for everyone except the poor sods on the receiving end.

Kit For heaven's sake, man, that was eight years ago! We were boys. At my age, I've neither the taste nor the energy for practical jokes.

Peter No, this wasn't a joke, was it — it was serious! You just can't stand people not doing as they're told! A quick twist of the valve and we're back in line!

Kit I ought to throw you out, Sims. But we made an agreement and, for Selena's sake, I'm prepared to see it through. Only get this straight — I did not touch your tyres!

Peter So perhaps you had another of your blackouts. You did what you wanted, without even knowing!

Kit How dare you! (*He advances towards Peter*)

Selena (*quickly stepping between them*) That's enough, Peter. I apologize, Kit. Peter's had a difficult day. Peter, Kit would never do such a thing.

Peter Well, if he didn't, how did it happen?

Kit I don't know. Local kids, perhaps, up from the village. We do get vandalism here.

Joe Or perhaps it's some of Terri's ghosts, hopped down off the balcony.

Peter Listen — Camberston didn't want us to go to the pub, and now we can't. He got his way.

Kit Nonsense. Of course you can go to the pub if you're that desperate. I've got a foot pump somewhere — in the stables, I think. I'll see if I can find it, while you try to calm down.

Kit exits

Selena Peter, you're outrageous.

Peter I don't care what he says, I still believe he hit the tyres. There's nothing those Hooray Henries like more than tormenting us peasants. Especially when we're trying to do a job of work.

Selena You're always fighting a class war that ended years ago!

Peter Don't you believe it! Those bastards'll still grind us down if we let them. Joe, I've rigged the generator on the roof, and dropped the cables down to the balcony. Find the best way to bring them through, and we're in business.

Joe OK, boss. (*He crosses and looks at the balcony doors and surrounds: then kneels to inspect lower down*) There's a ventilator here, goes right through, if I can get the grille out.

Peter Good, let's use that. Save keeping a window open.

Under the ensuing dialogue, Joe busies himself bringing cables in through a space near the floor, linking them up to the lamps and cameras, then setting up the lamps and the film camera

Selena Has it occurred to you that it was generous of Kit to let us come here?

Peter Don't kid yourself. He needs Crescent TV as much as we need Renfield House. He's getting a fat fee, right? He drove a pretty hard bargain.

Selena Not as much as Fain Castle would have cost.

Peter Enough. On top of that he's relying on "Paranormal" to put his dump on the map. It's his chance to make Renfield House a tourist trap.

Selena You think so?

Peter I know so. Once "Paranormal" is networked, he'll get trippers by the coach load. And he'll be set to take them for every penny!

Selena Well, why not? And anyway, how do you know that?

Peter A tip off from Jim Clay at Events Management. He thinks we should ask for a piece of the action. He says Camberston's looking for an organizer. A dogsbody to run everything while he takes the money.

Selena You really don't like him, do you?

Peter Oh, you noticed. No, I don't like him, or his kind of people. I hate the arrogance, the automatic assumption of authority, the condescension.

Selena I haven't seen any of that lately.

Peter What about this business with the poncy cold buffet?

Selena It was good of him to lay on food for us.

Peter He didn't lay it on, his servants did. And I turned it down politely enough. Why couldn't he just take no for an answer? Because his sort think an invitation from them is a royal command.

Selena Peter, you're being unreasonable.

Peter Am I? Well, I'll tell you something else I don't like, Selena. I don't like you taking Camberston's side all the time. You were glad enough to turn to me when he let you down. What about a little wifely support when war breaks out?

Selena For God's sake, Peter! Like I said, there isn't any war! We're all supposed to be working together on a programme! We need Kit's goodwill, as well as his house. He's got to do an interview, remember. We want him on our side, doing his best for "Paranormal".

Peter He'll do his best. I told you, it's his meal ticket.

Joe Did you bring the spare transformer, boss?

Peter No, d'you need it?

Joe I think I'm going to.

Peter You carry on; I'll get it from the van. And I want a word with Camberston. See if he's found that pump yet.

Selena You might apologize to him when you see him.

Peter I might. On the other hand, I might bend the foot pump over his conceited aristocratic head. He was going to the stables, wasn't he? Shouldn't be hard to find.

Peter exits

Selena Hm. Sorry about that. Creative tension, I think it's called.

Joe He won't need a foot pump, will he? Just put his mouth to the valve, and let off steam.

Terri I reckon that table will do for the séance, Selena. What do you think?

Selena It looks ancient enough. Have we got four chairs?

Terri (*glancing round at the furniture*) ... Three ... four. Yep. Not counting the one with the wobbly leg.

Joe Gawd! In this place, even the chairs walk with a limp.

Terri Joe, could you get the infra-red camera going? And the magnometer? They're mainly for the séance, but we could do some atmos tests in a minute.

Joe OK, why not?

Joe, having set up the lamps and the film camera, now tackles the other things. Selena finds a perch and checks the notes she made in the library

Joe You're really expecting to pick up a spook, aren't you?

Selena That's why we're here, Joe.

Terri For God's sake, we've picked one up already! It nearly brained you with the lamp!

Joe An accident, darling, like I said. Plus your imagination. Or wishful thinking.

Selena "There's nothing good or bad, but thinking makes it so."

Joe Right on, yeah. That's just what I meant. You put it very well.

Selena Actually, Shakespeare did.

Joe Shakespeare, eh? Well, that just shows great minds think alike. And I still say the lamp was rocky.

Terri It's not just the lamp, dumbo! There's huge psychic activity in here! I can sense it, I can smell it, I can almost touch it!

Joe Well, how come I can't feel a thing?

Terri Because you're not switched on.

Joe No-one's ever said that before.

Terri Not switched on to the right wavelength. It's like telly. The air's full of television signals, but you can't pick them up unless you've got a TV set — a receiver.

Selena But he nearly received a cracked skull. Look, I'm on your side, Terri. I want ghosts, we need them for the programme. But tell me, if you need a receiver to pick them up, how come a non-believer like Joe gets attacked?

Terri This is a ghost with a mission. An unquiet spirit.

Selena How does that happen?

Terri He or she is trapped. See, death is the moment when the body gives up everything. It happened to Somerset Maugham. You've heard of Somerset Maugham, Joe?

Joe Yes. Plays midfield for Yeovil, right?

Terri Somerset Maugham, the writer. Late in life, he died clinically twice on the operating table. Each time they managed to revive him.

Joe You don't get that on the National Health.

Terri When he was asked what death was like, he said it was the greatest orgasm he'd ever had.

Joe Gor! Well, that's something to look forward to. Why did I give up smoking?

Terri It's a letting go of everything — the soul, the spirit, memories, love, hate, all the emotions. The normal dead, the vast majority, let them go and move forward to the next stage of existence. But if something's held back, if someone tries to cling on to something unfinished — revenge, guilt, whatever — the process gets distorted. Their spirit's still anchored in this world, till the problem's solved.

Selena And that's what we've got here? A captive spirit? Restless? Frustrated?

Terri I'm sure of it. And maybe more than one. Caged — repressed — perhaps even vengeful. That's when they can turn malevolent, and strike out. (*Looking at Joe*) Especially at those who mock them.

Joe I didn't mock anyone. I was just getting on with the job.

Terri It was pretty obvious what you were thinking.

Joe Only to you, darling, 'cos you're a mind reader. You should have a tent at the fairground.

Terri Listen — I do not read minds, cards, palms or tea leaves. I communicate with dead people, not deadbeats.

Joe Anything you say, ma'am.

Terri You don't have to be a believer to work on this show, but you will need an open mind.

Joe I'll keep my mind so open, you'll hear the wind whistling through.

Kit enters

Kit I hope you're making progress.

Selena Yes, thanks. Did you find the foot pump?

Kit I've not only found it, I've blown up your tyres for you.

Selena Kit! That's very noble of you.

Kit Still got one good leg, you see. So now you can all drive down to the *Pear Tree* for hot pies and beer.

Joe Thanks, guv'nor.

Selena Did Peter see you?

Kit Not as far as I know. I certainly didn't see him. Should I have done?

Selena He went to look for you. He thought you'd be in the stables.

Kit No, I remembered the pump was in the outhouse.

Joe Did you pass the van? He was going to bring me some gear.

Kit The van? Yes, I was by the van just now. I pumped up the tyres, remember? And there was no sign of Peter Sims.

Joe Maybe he got there just before you did, saw some kids messing about, and chased off after them.

Selena More likely he's having a walk round, to clear his head. He'd worked himself into a pretty foul mood.

Kit Yes. I hope he's not always like that these days. And, if he's walking around the stables, he'll need to be careful. There's no moon tonight.

Terri And there's an oubliette out there.

Kit Precisely. I hope he's got a torch.

Terri No, he hasn't. I've got the Crescent TV torch. (*She gropes in her rucksack and produces a torch*) Look, I've done all I can for now, and I'd be glad of a break from this room. I think I'll go out and look for Peter. OK with you, Selena?

Selena As long as you take Joe with you. I don't want a girl walking around alone out there in the dark. Can you break off, Joe?

Joe Sure. I need that transformer from the van anyway.

Joe and Terri head for the door. Joe puts his arm around Terri

Come on, darling. If we're not back in four hours, call the Vice Squad.

Joe and Terri exit

Selena I'm glad of a chance to talk to you alone, Kit. I want to say sorry for Peter's behaviour.

Kit Thank you, Selena, but it's not your fault.

Selena Well, in a way it is. You realize, of course, that Peter's wildly jealous about our past relationship?

Kit Jealous? Why should he be jealous? He came out the winner.

Selena Only because you made an ass of yourself. For him, it's like winning a tennis match 'cos your opponent sprains his wrist when he's leading. I'm afraid Peter has a vast inferiority complex where you're concerned.

Kit Extraordinary. A successful TV producer, with a glamorous wife and a first-class degree, feels inferior to an unemployed jail-bird? A man who got chucked out of college?

Selena Kit …

Kit He's over-awed by a dried-out drunk with no qualifications and a limp?

Selena Don't be naïve, Kit. It's a question of background. Did you know Peter was brought up in a two room council flat in Bermondsey?

Kit It doesn't surprise me.

Selena He had to work like mad to get to University. Then, when he got there, he found a few chaps like you ruling the roost — young gods who'd had all the good things of life just drop into their laps.

Kit Including losing both parents when I was eighteen?

Selena I did mention that to him once. He didn't actually say so, but I think he felt that rich people who fly to the West Indies on holiday expect to have the odd plane crash.

Kit I'm afraid I can't find that reaction very endearing.

Selena But, to answer your question earlier — no, Peter isn't always like that. He's normally quiet, hard-working and even- tempered. Sometimes he's actually quite amusing. I'm afraid you've got him at a bad time.

Kit You mean, while he's alive.

Selena You might as well know, Kit, it's been a difficult year. Crescent TV is in trouble.

Kit I thought you said you'd done well?

Selena Well, in this business, you always act successful. But now I want to explain Peter's attitude, even if I can't excuse it.

Kit You mean, he's anxious about the business.

Selena He's been worried sick for months. We've a massive overdraft and a huge bank loan we've no hope of paying off unless "Paranormal" is a hit.

Kit Good Lord! I'd no idea. How did this happen? What about all those programmes you mentioned?

Selena "Exploring Britain" did quite well. Well enough to make us expand, which was a big mistake. Buying equipment instead of hiring it, and then watching our stuff get out of date.

Kit And the cookery series?

Selena Could have done well, if there hadn't been three other cookery programmes on the same night. Our chef wasn't as weird as the others, so we got axed.

Kit Oh dear. Can they do that?

Selena Of course. You're in the hands of network bosses. And, thanks to that disaster, we've not been able to sell our science series. Now our house is mortgaged and the bank's nearly ready to foreclose.

Kit Selena! I'm so sorry!

Selena I shouldn't have mentioned it. But, after Peter's behaviour, I thought you deserved an explanation.

Kit Thanks. This must be a nightmare for you.

Selena Not so much for me. I've been doing freelance work for other people.

Kit But the finance. You told me Crescent TV's a joint venture.

Selena Yes. But I'm not a worrier. I kept my old flat on, rented out. If we lose the house we can go back there. And I've always got my career. The Beeb would give me a contract anytime. It's different for Peter. Producers and directors are only as good as their last show.

Kit It's a tough world.

Selena The toughest. Once backers lose confidence, you can't get the funds. Now you know why Peter's a worried man.

Kit Yes. I'll try to make allowances. I know a bit about slings and arrows from my own experience.

Selena Indeed you do. And maybe I wasn't quite as sympathetic as I might have been.

Kit Well ... I brought my troubles on myself, didn't I? It's hard to be sympathetic when someone's been a bloody fool.

Selena (*with forced brightness*) Anyway, "Paranormal" will be a winner and all our troubles will be over.

Kit I'll do all I can to help, I promise you.

Selena And I'm sure your ghosts will do the same. Terri's convinced this room is teeming with psychic activity.

Kit It's not just this room, you know. My great-grandfather swore there were malevolent spirits surrounding the house.

Selena I saw that in his notes. There was something in the stables, wasn't there? Where the groom used to work?

Kit Apparently. Of course, there have been no horses here for years. But, when we did have them, it seems they used to bolt for no reason. A normally placid mare once kicked a stable boy and broke his ankle. And then there were a couple of fires.

Selena I reckon we could get half a dozen programmes out of this place. Once we've got the pilot right.

Joe rushes in, looking worried

Joe Hey, there's something wrong! There's blood in the van!

Kit Blood?

Joe In the van. I didn't see Peter, so I went straight to the van, to get the transformer. And there's blood on the dashboard!

Kit How could you tell in the dark?

Joe I put my hand there, while I was reaching inside. It was all sticky. When I got indoors I saw why. (*He holds up his left hand. There's a big smear of blood on the palm*)

Selena My God! Where's Terri?

Joe I don't know, we split up. She took the torch to look for Peter in the stables. I went to the van, and there was all this blood!

Selena What the hell's going on? First Peter disappears! Now Terri!

Kit Keep calm! He didn't say she'd disappeared, he just said they'd split up. She'll still be out looking for Peter.

Selena But the blood! Where did the blood come from?

Kit We'll have to find out, won't we?

Selena And where's my husband?

Kit Like you said, he probably took a walk to cool off. And Terri's trying to find him.

Joe Yeah. They'll both be blundering around in the dark.

Kit I think I can find a torch downstairs. Come with me, young man, and we'll comb the area.

Joe OK, guv'nor.

Selena I should come too.

Kit No, Selena, you can do better than that. Does Peter carry a mobile phone?

Selena Always. It's on his belt.

Kit Have you got one?

Selena Yes. In my bag.

Kit Good. Then you just ring him, and find out where he is, and what he's up to.

Selena Right. If I can find the number. I can never remember these long mobile numbers.

Kit Try. (*He moves towards the door*) Don't worry, we'll soon find both of them.

Kit and Joe exit

Left alone, Selena gets her mobile and her diary from her handbag. She looks in the diary for Peter's number

A faint scent of violets permeates the theatre, and the temperature on the thermometer is falling

Selena (*finding the number she wants*) Ah!

Selena punches the number up on her mobile. There is no response from the other end. She calls Peter's name several times into the phone, but there's still no response. The silence lasts for several seconds: then, suddenly, the phone lets out an ear-piercing screech. Selena reels back, and drops the phone

The Lights flicker and fade during the following

A window slams shut, off. The room door closes with a bang. Selena rushes across and tries to pull the door open, but it won't budge

Now we hear the piano playing, as before, and the sound of the woman sobbing. Behind the sobbing and the sound of the piano, the Lights finally go out altogether. There are a few moments of sobbing, piano and darkness. Then, suddenly, one of the TV spotlights comes on, brilliantly illuminating the portrait of Philomel on the rear wall. There is a gash across Philomel's throat with blood oozing from it

Selena stares at the picture in horror, then gasps and faints

A moment's silence follows, and then there's an unearthly female scream as ——

— *the* CURTAIN *falls*

ACT II

The same. Fifteen minutes later

The TV spotlight is off and the Tower Room is in darkness. The blood and the gash have gone from Philomel's portrait. Selena lies where she fell

The door handle is rattled, but the door is stuck. It is buffeted from the outside two or three times before it opens, and three figures enter: Kit, with a torch, leading the way, followed by Terri and Joe. Kit is now using a different walking-stick from that used in Act I

Kit I've never known that door to stick before ... Hallo, what's happened? The place is dark.
Terri Where's Selena?

Kit switches on the room light, and they see Selena lying on the floor

Kit She's on the floor!

They hurry to her aid. Kit picks her up and lays her on the chaise-longue. She regains consciousness during the following. Kit kneels by her and tries to comfort her

Terri Is she all right?
Kit I think so. She's breathing normally. She must have fainted. Fetch a glass of brandy, will you — er — Joe? There are glasses and a bottle on the sideboard in the drawing-room downstairs.
Joe Can I make that two, guv'nor? It was a bit cold out there.
Kit Of course. Help yourself to anything. Bring the bottle.
Joe Ta.

Joe exits

Kit Selena, are you all right? What's the matter? What happened?

Selena murmurs and moves, and then is suddenly alert, aware of the horrors she experienced

Selena The blood! The blood! On the picture! It's bleeding!

Kit (*gently*) A picture bleeding? What are you talking about, my dear? Which picture was this?

Selena Over there! The picture of Philomel!

Kit and Terri look at the picture

Kit The picture isn't bleeding, Selena. It must have been an illusion. Anyway, the light was out.

Selena Yes, yes, it went out. But then another light came on. Very bright. It lit up that picture. And Philomel was bleeding, where her throat had been cut!

Terri (*making notes*) Are you sure you saw this?

Selena Of course I'm sure! And the piano was playing. And I could hear someone sobbing. You're right, Terri. This room is as haunted as hell!

Terri God! The whole place is coming alive!

Selena I just wish it could have waited till·we were ready.

Terri Did you smell violets?

Selena Yes, I did. And the temperature dropped.

Terri The room's been deserted so long, the spirits were starved of contact. Now someone's aroused them. It must be you, Selena.

Selena I hope not. I wouldn't want to go through that again — at least, not on my own. It was terrifying. Suddenly the door slammed, and I was trapped.

Kit The door is easily explained. The wind got up twenty minutes ago.

Selena But the door wouldn't open! I pulled it and pulled it, and it was stuck fast!

Kit It was jammed when we got here. It just needed a big push from the other side.

Joe enters with a bottle of brandy and two glasses. He pours a glass of brandy and gives it to Kit, who puts it to Selena's lips

Kit Drink this, Selena. Brandy. Only three star, but it'll make you feel better.

Selena Thanks. Where's Peter? Have you found Peter?

Kit Not yet, I'm afraid. You didn't get him on your mobile?

Selena No. I dialled his number, but all I got was silence, and then the most hideous shriek.

Kit I suppose that's better than the dreadful recorded woman telling you the line's busy.

Terri I expect Peter's phone's off. He'll be sitting down somewhere, trying to get his head straight.

Selena But for so long!

Kit Well, at least we found your researcher. And she tells me he carries a hip flask of Scotch. So he may be seeking a little consolation. Does that ever happen?

Selena It has been known. But what about the blood in the van?

Kit Ah, that turns out to be a false alarm.

Terri My fault, Selena. I should have told someone. When we were unloading, I cut my finger on a sharp edge, and started bleeding like a stuck pig. I must have left blood on the dashboard, when I got the First Aid kit from the glove compartment. (*She holds up a hand, with a large plaster on one finger*)

Selena Oh. You didn't rest your hand on that portrait, I suppose?

Terri No, sorry, that's not so easily explained. There are a lot of things we shan't understand till we hold the séance. I think we should start.

Selena Hang on, we can't hold the séance without Peter.

Terri Why not? Joe can work the cameras and the sound recorder runs itself. We've got to tap this dynamism while it's in full flood!

Joe Excuse me, but what about our break?

Terri We can't go to the pub without Peter. He'd turn up and find the van gone!

Joe I need to eat!

Kit If you get hungry enough, young man, you might be reduced to eating some of the cold buffet downstairs. And I believe I may have some lager in the cellar.

Joe Oh ... ta.

Selena Sorry, Joe, the pub's off till Peter's here. Kit, I'm really worried. Should we ring the police?

Kit And tell them what? That your husband went off in a huff and hasn't been seen for an hour? I don't think they'd be very pleased.

Terri I'm sure Peter's all right. Remember that time we were making "Science For You"? He had that row with Jeff Farrell and disappeared for two hours! It turned out he'd been walking the streets, kicking lamp-posts.

Selena There are no lamp-posts here to kick!

Terri So he'll be walking round kicking the trees.

Selena I'd like to think so. But so many strange things are happening.

Terri Listen, if you think something strange has happened to Peter, something to do with the haunting, then the séance is the way to find out. There are spirits that know everything. For God's sake, let's do it!

Selena It doesn't seem right. This is Peter's project.

Terri And yours. And mine.

Selena OK, but he's the main man. And the séance is the main mission. It's bizarre to do it without him.

Terri All right. Let's call this a dummy run. Film it, and Peter can see what we've got. If he wants another séance, we can do it. These spirits won't leave in a hurry. But, if we don't respond soon, they could get dangerous.

Selena Can you handle it on your own, Joe?

Joe Yeah, sure. The sooner we get this done, the sooner I get to eat.

Selena Very well, let's go ahead, it's better than just waiting. Terri, you take charge of the séance, Joe — handle the filming.

Joe busies himself with lining up cameras and setting recording equipment et cetera, under the ensuing dialogue

Terri Right, Selena, let's have you at the table here. I'd like you here, and Sir Christopher there, with me in the middle.

Kit Have I got to be involved in this?

Terri Absolutely. I need a circle of at least three. And, as a Camberston, you're essential.

Kit (*sighing*) Then it seems I have no option.

Serena, Terri and Kit take their places at the table. There is an empty fourth chair, the one intended for Peter. Joe gets in position by the camera

Terri (*holding the locket*) Now then ... I want calm ... I want silence. It's obvious that the unquiet spirits in this room arise from its tragic history — from the murder that happened here a hundred and fifty years ago — the murder of Philomel. I want us all to think of Philomel ... Look at her portrait ... Think of Philomel ... Think of Philomel. (*Pause*) Philomel, I have your locket here, it's beautiful. Philomel, come and admire your locket. (*Pause*) Are you there, Philomel? Is it you who plays the piano? Play it for us now. (*Pause*) Are you there, Philomel? Is anyone there? (*Pause*) There is someone there, isn't there. Come to me ... Speak to me ... We are your friends. (*Pause*) There is someone there! There's a noise! A murmuring!

Joe (*behind the camera*) That's my gut rumbling! It's empty!

Selena Joe! How dare you? Shut up, this is serious.

Joe Sorry. Sorry. Couldn't resist it.

Terri You fool! We've driven a hundred miles to contact these spirits, and now you want to spoil everything!

Joe Sorry. I won't do it again.

Terri You'd better not. Can I have silence again, please? Please all concentrate on this room — on the tragedy — on the murder — on this locket. Everyone concentrate ... Concentrate ... Philomel, here's your locket — and there's your piano. If you're here, let us have a sign ... Speak through me. Philomel? Philomel? (*Pause*) Philomel, have you brought violets? I can smell violets. Philomel, I know you're there! Speak through me, and then perhaps you can rest.

The piano is heard, playing softly. It continues under the following

Kit My God! It's happening!
Selena But it's cold! So cold!
Terri Quiet! Philomel, you play as beautifully as ever. Your spirit is here with me! I know it! (*In surprise*) There's another spirit here! There's another spirit! Who are you? What do you want to say? (*Pause*) You empathize with someone here, don't you. Someone of your kin is here! Speak through them, spirit! Speak to us through your kin!

There's a moment's silence and then Joe, behind the camera, begins to moan ecstatically

Selena Joe, don't be stupid! No more clowning!
Terri (*with sudden huge excitement*) He's not clowning! He's possessed! The spirit's in him!

Joe drops down on one knee, still moaning ecstatically. After a few seconds, he stops moaning, and looks up in horror. At the same time, the piano stops, with a crashing discord. Joe gets to his feet, in deadly fear, and starts to cry out in an English rural accent

Joe Oh no! No! It's him! He's come back! No, don't touch her, you monster, you've hurt her enough! It's not her fault, it's mine! Oh God, have mercy! … Aagh!

Joe clutches his chest, as if shot, groans in agony, and falls back into the vacant chair, where he sits, shaking and sobbing

Selena moves towards Joe

Selena Joe! Joe! Are you all right?
Terri Leave him alone! Don't wake him! I told you, he's possessed! The spirit's taken him over!
Joe Murder! Murder! Aagh!

Joe is jerked back, as if by another blow. He writhes in agony

Selena But for God's sake! Shouldn't we get him out of it?

Terri No! He'd suffer brain damage! Let it take its course. It'll leave when it's ready.

Joe (*still in a trance, but suddenly animated again*) Tell them the truth! Tell them the truth!

Terri The spirit's got something to say. It won't go till it's said!

Joe Such wickedness! Such evil! You never loved her! You evil man! I'll tell the truth, and then you'll hang. (*He struggles for breath, as if being strangled*)

Selena He can't breathe!

Terri Leave him! This is amazing! There's another spirit here! Yet another spirit! Evil! Some dark force, trying to silence him!

Selena But Joe! It sounds like he's dying!

Terri He won't die. The voice'll get through. It always does.

Joe (*as if shaking off strangling hands*) I will speak! I will speak! I'll tell the truth! About him! And about her! And about me!

Kit leaps up and pounces on Joe, grabbing him by the throat

Kit (*in a different voice, now very strong and fierce*) You'll say no more, you insolent oaf! Not another word, d'you hear? Not another word! Not ever!

Selena Kit! What on earth are you doing?

Kit Vile scoundrel! Ungrateful wretch! Watch the adultress die! And then I'll finish you!

Terri This is dangerous. We'll have to get him off!

Terri grabs Kit's arm. Selena joins in, and the two women pull Kit off Joe. Both men collapse, semi-conscious, into their chairs

Terri That's enough, you spirits! Go now! Go in peace! (*She slumps back, exhausted*)

Selena Wow! Is it over, Terri?

Terri I think so. For the moment, at least. The spirits have spoken. They may be satisfied.

Selena Did all that mean what I thought it meant?

Terri It looks pretty obvious. Selena, you were reading about the murder. How did the groom, Hunte, spell his name?

Selena I noticed because it was unusual. There was an "e" on the end.

Terri Did you know Joe's surname is Hunte? With an "e" on the end?

Selena Good God! You think Joe is related to the groom?

Terri A direct descendant, I should think, judging from what we just heard. It was Joe's arrival that summoned his ancestor's spirit. Set the whole thing off.

Selena Why did it bring the lamp down on him?

Terri If it did. We don't know. More likely it was the other spirit, the one that wanted to stop him. What is clear is that, for a century and a half, Paul Hunte has wanted the truth to be known.

Selena The truth. Which is …?

Terri I'm sure you've worked it out for yourself. Hunte didn't murder Philomel, her husband did. Hunte and Philomel must have been lovers. Sir Richard caught them at it, and killed them both. Shot Hunte and then cut his wife's throat, while the groom was dying.

Joe sits up, shaking his head. Selena goes to the brandy bottle, pours some into a glass, and takes it to him

Selena It's all over, Joe. I hope you left the camera running. Drink some brandy.

Joe (*returning to his normal voice*) Thanks.

Selena Are you yourself again?

Joe Yeah. Yeah, I think so. That was weird. I didn't know what I was doing till the guy started throttling me. What was he on about? Is he OK?

Terri He has blackouts at the best of times. This must have brought on a big one.

Joe I heard you talking to Selena — saying what you think happened.

Terri Does it make sense to you?

Joe Yeah, yeah, I guess so. I could be kin to that groom. Both my pa and grandpa were into horses. Mainly losing money on them. Was that bloke trying to kill me?

Terri I think that was the general idea. But he didn't know what he was doing. He was taken over, just like you were.

Joe Yeah. But it never happened to me before. If this guy has a lot of blackouts, he could be attacking people and never know it.

Terri He could, but I doubt it. Just now it was his ancestor trying to kill your ancestor. Sir Christopher's got no reason to kill anyone, so far as I know.

Selena So Sir Richard's spirit haunts the room, as well as Paul Hunte.

Terri Looks like it. Maybe now they've said their piece they'll go.

Selena And if not?

Terri Sir Christopher could call in an exorcist. At least now they'll know what they're up against.

Selena Amazing that it was two men. And we all thought it was Philomel.

Terri Don't rule out Philomel. My instinct tells me there's more to this than Hunte and Camberston.

Kit (*stirring; in his normal voice*) Who's there? What's happening? When are you going to start the séance?

Selena pours brandy into the second glass and takes it to Kit

Selena Your turn with the brandy, I think. We've had the séance, Kit. With pretty sensational results.

Kit You've had the séance? I must have fallen asleep. What happened?

Selena Rather a lot.

Terri You don't remember trying to strangle Joe here?

Kit What? I've never tried to strangle anyone in my life.

Terri I thought so. Sir Christopher, you were possessed by the spirit of your ancestor, Sir Richard. Using you, he tried to silence the spirit of Paul Hunte, the murdered groom.

Kit Murdered groom? It was he who murdered Philomel, wasn't it?

Terri No. It seems Sir Richard murdered both Philomel and Hunte. For years, Hunte's spirit has wanted to put the record straight. And Sir Richard's spirit has sought to restrain him. Hence the conflict in this room.

Kit This is all gobbledegook, as far as I'm concerned. Give me more brandy, will you, Selena? I'm feeling very vulnerable, very strange. There's an alien presence in this room.

Terri No, no, the spirits are quiet now. The message has been delivered.

Kit (*agitatedly*) There is someone — something — here, I tell you! Something malevolent! I can sense it! I can hear it! It's coming closer!

Peter's hand, white and smeared with blood, appears round the door post

Selena lets out a shriek

For a moment Peter clings to the door post from the outside, then, dishevelled, with blood on his face and hands and mud on his trousers, he stumbles into the room and collapses as ——

—— the CURTAIN *falls*

SCENE 2

The same. Two minutes later

When the CURTAIN *rises Peter is sitting in a chair, and Terri is examining the back of his head. The others hover anxiously*

Terri Nasty bruise ... Quite a small cut, probably won't need stitches ... (*She turns her attention to his forehead*)

Selena Shouldn't he go to hospital?

Peter (*gasping for breath*) No, no, we haven't time. I could do with a clean-up though.

Kit There's a bathroom on the next floor down.

Terri There's a bruise on the forehead, too, with quite a large graze. How on earth did all this happen?

Peter I was on my way to the stables to find Camberston. Someone hit me from behind — then pushed me down the oubliette. I must have hit my forehead as I fell.

Selena You went down the oubliette? How the hell did you get out?

Peter Obviously no-one's cleared it out since the Middle Ages. It's three quarters full of mud and muck and leaves. (*He brushes mud off his trousers*) Not very nice to land on, but it broke my fall. Come to think of it, there must be a few ancient bones under that lot.

Kit Were you conscious?

Peter No, I was out for a while. When I came to, I rested to get my strength back, and think what to do. Then I discovered that the stonework's crumbling. There were hand holds and foot holds. Eventually I managed to climb up and out.

Selena Thank God!

Peter Yes. I wasn't meant to. That blow was intended to kill me.

Selena We must tell the police at once.

Peter No, no. Like I said, we haven't time. There's no permanent damage. I'd rather not mess about answering questions from PC Plod.

Selena But this was an assault! Attempted murder!

Peter Also, I don't think we want you to go to jail again, Camberston, for Selena's sake. Better if we hush this up, and you see a psychiatrist.

Kit Me? See a psychiatrist? What the devil are you talking about?

Peter It was you who attacked me, wasn't it? But I'm prepared to believe you had one of your blackouts.

Kit How dare you? I've had a few blackouts since my illness, but I've never harmed anyone.

Peter If you're blacked out, you don't know, do you?

Terri He attacked Joe just now. If we hadn't pulled him off, he'd have throttled him.

Kit That's what *you* say. I wasn't aware of any of that.

Joe Well, I was. And I've got the marks to prove it. (*He rubs his painful neck*)

Peter You say he attacked Joe as well?

Selena He was possessed, Peter. We've just had the most astonishing séance. Terri called up the spirits, and the whole truth came out.

Peter You've had the séance without me?

Selena We didn't want to, but we had to act quickly. We've got some amazing scenes on film.

Peter And what is the truth?

Selena The groom wasn't the killer. He and Philomel were lovers, Sir Richard murdered them both.

Kit This is wild speculation!

Peter Sounds convincing to me. It seems violence runs in the family.

Kit Look, I've had enough of this! You come here as my guests, you insult me, and abuse my hospitality. Then you blacken my family's name, and now you suggest I'm a homicidal maniac!

Peter It's no use denying the attack, Camberston. You've always hated me because I took Selena from you.

Selena Look, must we have all this? ...

Peter Camberston has to face facts. (*To Kit*) When you blacked out, your instincts took over. You saw a chance to kill me, and you took it.

Kit (*now really angry*) Lies! Lies! How dare you say these things! It's slanderous nonsense!

Peter I don't think so. When I crawled out of that bloody hole I found this on the ground, where I was attacked.

Peter produces from his pocket the silver knob seen earlier on Kit's walking stick, and holds it up

Kit Clever of you to spot it in the dark.

Peter I stumbled over it. It's the knob from your walking stick, isn't it? I see you're now using a different one.

Selena (*to Kit*) Is that really off your stick?

Kit Probably. It disappeared a while ago. I've no doubt someone wrenched it off for their own purposes.

Peter (*still holding up the silver knob*) Leave it out, Camberston. That knob came off when you hit me. It's got my blood on it. Get yourself to a psychiatrist quick, before you kill someone!

Kit snatches the knob and hurls it to the ground in a fury

Kit That's enough! That's more than enough! I want you out of my house at once, do you hear? All of you! At once! Pack up your wretched things and go!

Selena Kit, I'm sorry about all this. Please be patient, I'm sure we can work something out ...

Kit I'm sorry too, Selena, sorry about the company you keep. Well, I don't have to be involved any more. You heard me, Sims. Get your crew and your equipment out of here! And get your infernal van off my land! Within the hour — or I'll call the police and have you evicted!

Kit storms out

Peter (*disgustedly*) He'll call the police! And I just spared him an assault charge!

Terri It's all right, Peter, we've got enough material for a sensational programme. Lucky we shot those exteriors earlier.

Peter No interview, of course, but Selena can tell the whole story to camera. And maybe talk to some psychic expert.

Selena Why not Terri? They don't come more psychic than her!

Peter Fine, we can do that back in London. Well, so be it. I've certainly no wish to stay in Renfield House any longer. (*He rubs the back of his head*) I've got quite enough to remember it by.

Selena Are you all right, Peter?

Peter Yes, I'm OK. I've got a pretty thick skull. But I will go and get cleaned up. Joe, Terri, will you start shifting the gear?

Joe OK, boss. I shan't be sorry to go either. That Camberston bloke's crazy as a loon!

Peter exits

Joe sets to work disconnecting things. Terri gathers up small items of equipment

Selena Joe, we haven't time to run the film. Just guard it with your life. But could you check the sound monitor worked?

Joe Sure. Why not?

Joe goes to the recording machine, switches on, and a recording of the séance begins, playing low under the following dialogue

Yeah, we got it.

Selena Thank God. Joe, will you help me listen to it for a minute?

Joe *Help* you listen?

Selena I might ask for some adjustments to the sound. The professional touch.

Joe OK. No problem.

Terri I'll start taking things to the van.

Selena Borrow my coat, Terri, it's cold out there.

Terri Thanks. (*She puts on the Crescent TV jacket*) Let's get away soon. There's still evil in this place. I've got a feeling something terrible could happen.

Terri picks up some pieces of equipment and leaves

Selena listens closely to the séance recording

Selena Can you turn it up, Joe?

Joe increases the volume so that Terri and the others are clearly audible, and some background noise as well

Joe That loud enough?
Selena For the moment. (*She listens intently*) Listen to the background. Something extra. Can you hear a woman?
Joe Yeah, I can hear Terri. She's a whole lot of woman.
Selena Apart from Terri. Can you hear a woman crying?
Joe (*listening intently*) Yeah. Yeah, I think I can.
Selena Can you bring up the bass a bit?

Joe adjusts a knob, and more bass is audible. With the bass comes the sobbing sound we heard before

Joe Yeah, that's weird! This is getting too creepy for me. I should have taken that job on the pop video!
Selena Quiet! It's Philomel, I'm sure. The men create all the drama, and she just cries her heart out. Poor Philomel. I think she's in this room all the time. Listen carefully — get a bit more bass if you can.

Joe adjusts again, the bass comes up a little more and then, suddenly, on the tape there comes the hideous screech we heard earlier. After that, the tape goes silent

What the hell was that? That's the screech I heard on my mobile!
Joe And what's happened to the sound?
Selena Is the tape turning?
Joe Yeah. And the volume needle's still flickering on "High".
Selena Please God the tape's not wiped.
Joe No, look, that needle means the tape's still putting out sound. But for some reason we're not hearing it. I'll switch off and check the speaker. (*He switches off the machine and studies its innards*)

Selena peers intently at the machine

There is an eerie silence. It is shattered by the loud sound of a gunshot outside, quickly followed by another. Selena and Joe, aghast, look towards the windows

Holy Moses! What's happening here?
Selena That sounded like gunshots!
Joe Those were gunshots all right. Right outside the house. (*He moves to the balcony doors*) Hey, d'you think Camberston's gone crazy with a gun?

Selena Joe, stay away from the windows! Someone out there could shoot you!

Joe stops short of the balcony, but is able to open one of the doors slightly and peer out

Joe Can't see nothing. It's too dark.

Selena moves towards the room door

Hey, where are you going?
Selena To find out what's happened.
Joe Are you insane? There could be a madman out there with a gun. We've got to keep him out, not go down and join him! (*Seeing a bolt on the inside of the door*) Hey, there's a bolt here! (*He slides the bolt home*)
Selena Someone may be shot. We can't just stay here.
Joe We can till we know what's going on.
Selena I'm thinking of Peter. And Terri.
Joe I'm thinking of you. And me, come to think of it. My mum's only got ten kids. She can't afford to lose one.
Selena But for God's sake! Peter or Terri may be hurt. We can't just do nothing!
Joe Look, someone out there's got a gun, right? And we're unarmed!
Selena We don't have to be. There must be something here we can use as weapons.

Selena and Joe look round the junk that's been stored in the tower room, and Selena's eye quickly lights on a pair of Indian clubs

Over here, look. Indian clubs. One each.
Joe Yeah. When I took this job, no-one said I'd have to fight off a bleeding gunman with a poxy bit of wood.

Nevertheless, Joe picks up a club, as does Selena, and both move towards the door. As they approach, the handle turns and someone tries to open the door from the outside. For a moment, Selena and Joe stand frozen. Now the person outside bangs repeatedly on the door and, after a moment, we hear his voice

Peter (*off*) Joe! Terri! It's Peter! Let me in, for God's sake! It's Peter. Let me in! Terri, are you in there?
Selena (*calling*) All right, Peter! Don't push! We've got to move a bolt.

Joe slides the bolt

The door opens and Peter bursts in. He's now cleaned up, but extremely agitated. He's astonished to see Selena

Peter Selena! You're here! Thank God! But I don't understand.

Selena Of course I'm here. Why wouldn't I be?

Peter Camberston's gone berserk! He's got a gun! I saw him shoot you as you stood by the van!

Joe Selena didn't go to the van.

Selena Oh God, d'you see what happened? I lent my coat to Terri! Terri went down there wearing my coat!

Peter So it's Terri the bastard's shot! Poor girl, I wasn't close enough to see her face. I just saw the coat, in the light from the window. And Camberston made the same mistake!

Joe You reckon he meant to kill Selena?

Peter It's obvious. He hates us all, but me and Selena the most. He's gone completely mad!

Joe I guess we'd better bolt this door again. (*He slides the bolt closed*)

Selena What happened, Peter?

Peter Poor Terri, she went down like a ninepin. She's crumpled by the van.

Selena You didn't go to help her?

Peter How could I? Camberston was standing there, ready to shoot. I wouldn't have stood a chance.

Joe Where were you, boss?

Peter I'd just gone out of the front door. I saw the figure by the van and I thought it was Selena. As I stepped outside, Camberston came from the stables with a gun. He just took aim and shot her. Then he fired at me as I dashed back in.

Selena Where's Kit now?

Peter Still outside, I hope. I slammed the front door and bolted it.

Selena It won't take him long to get in. Call 999 on your mobile. Mine doesn't work here, but yours might.

Peter Of course … Yes …

Peter snatches the mobile from his belt and taps out 999. Nothing happens. He tries once more. Again, nothing. Joe tries to peer through the window without getting too close to it

Peter (*giving up*) No good. Nothing. There's no signal in this blasted place.

Selena Try the main phone, downstairs.

Peter First thing I did. That's dead, too. Camberston must have cut the wires.

Selena And poor Terri's still lying there!

Peter Joe and I will have to go for help.

Joe What? Go out there?

Peter Yes, of course go out there! With two of us, we might confuse him. Especially as it's Selena he's after. One of us should get through.

Selena Peter! This is crazy!

Peter It's the only way. Better than waiting for him to blast his way in, and pick us off one by one!

Joe I don't know. He might not bother with me.

Peter Listen — we can't leave Terri on the ground, bleeding to death!

Selena What's the plan then?

Peter When we're ready, you hold this door open. Joe and I charge out, and keep running till we reach the van. When we get there, Joe, you open both the doors, we pick up Terri and put her inside. Then we both get in and drive like hell!

Joe I've got a feeling I'm not going to make that party on Saturday.

Selena Course you will, and you'll be a hero. The girls'll be all over you!

Peter We'll reach the village in five minutes. There'll be phones there — perhaps even a police station. We'll have help here in fifteen minutes. You just have to stay barricaded that long in here, Selena.

Selena I should come with you!

Peter Don't be silly, it's you he's after. By now he'll have found out it wasn't you he shot.

Selena But why? Why does he want to kill me?

Peter Resentment — jealousy — or just plain insanity. Believe me, this is the safest place.

Selena But I'll be alone!

Peter For fifteen minutes. With luck, Camberston won't even be back in the house yet. This room's got a good stout door. Once we're out, pile furniture against it. And pray!

Selena I'll be praying.

Peter Right. Come on, Joe. Bring that club with you. Open the door, Selena.

Joe picks up the club, and the two men get ready to charge

Selena (*as she tentatively opens the door*) Let's hope he's not waiting outside.

The door is now wide open

Peter OK, Joe ... go!

The men charge out

Selena quickly shuts the door behind them and bolts it. Then she jams a chair against the door handle. She augments this with other furniture and, when that's done, she stops and looks around. She finds herself drawn to the sound recording machine again. She moves across and switches it on. The tape makes no sound. She spools it back to the start, activates it afresh, and now we hear the séance again, more quietly this time

The door handle is turned, and an attempt is made to open the door from the outside

Selena freezes, then switches off the machine and watches the door in terror

Kit (*off; friendly and coaxing*) Selena, are you there? What have you done to the door? Selena?

There's another rattle of the handle and another vain attempt to open the door

Selena, are you all right? Why won't you let me in? The others have gone now. Don't you want to see me? Selena? (*Pause. His voice moving away from the door*) Oh well, I'll come back later and see if you've changed your mind.

All is silent

Selena sets to work to reinforce the barricade at the door, then breaks off and tries dialling 999 on her mobile, but with no success. Carrying her Indian club, she looks for more furniture for the door. This move brings her close to the balcony doors, but in a blind spot where she cannot be seen from the balcony

A balcony door opens and Kit enters, carrying a shotgun

Kit (*as he enters; calling*) Selena! Selena, where are you? Why have you bolted the door?

Selena finds herself behind Kit, unseen, with a club in her hand. She crashes it down on the back of his head, and he falls unconscious. Selena looks down at Kit for a moment, and then decides to get away fast. She rushes across the room and removes the furniture from the door. As soon as the door is cleared, she unbolts it and flings it open

And there stands Peter. He seems strangely calm and rather sinister

Peter Hallo, Selena.

Selena Peter! Thank heavens you're here!

Selena throws herself into Peter's arms

Kit got in, but I hit him with a club. I managed to knock him out.

Peter disentangles himself and looks across at Kit lying on the floor by the balcony

Peter So you did. Well done, my darling. Ah yes, the steps from the roof —
we forgot about that way in. Still, it seems you coped rather well.
Selena I thought you and Joe were going off in the van.
Peter Just as we got Terri in, I thought I heard you scream.
Selena Me? I didn't scream.
Peter Brave girl. Anyway, I thought you did, and I came to rescue you.
Selena Where's Joe?
Peter I sent him off without me. Don't worry, help will be here soon.
Selena How's Terri?
Peter Bad news, I'm afraid. She must have died instantly. These hunting
types usually shoot straight.
Selena Poor girl. Let's get out of here, Peter. We can wait for the police
downstairs.
Peter Better take Camberston's gun. We don't want him grabbing that when
he wakes up. (*He walks over to where Kit lies, his gun by his side*) Oh,
Selena …
Selena Yes, darling?
Peter Could you spool back the séance tape, and lift it out? I want it with me.
Selena Couldn't we come back and collect all the stuff when the police are
here?
Peter Most of it, but I want to be sure of that tape. If Camberston comes to
while we're downstairs, he might destroy it out of spite.
Selena All right, only let's not hang about. I've seen enough of this room to
last me a lifetime. (*She bends over the machine and spools the tape, with
her back to Peter*)

*Peter takes a pair of thick cotton gloves from his pocket, dons them, and picks
up Kit's gun. Then he points the gun carefully at the back of Selena's head,
and pulls the trigger*

*There's a loud click. Selena is alerted and swings round. She is astonished
to see her husband pointing the gun at her*

Peter Damn! He's taken the shells out!
Selena Peter! What on earth are you doing?

Peter I'm afraid I have to kill you, Selena.

Selena Kill me? What are you talking about?

Peter Oh hell. I hate boring explanations. All your troubles should be over by now, my dear. But since your wretched boyfriend saw fit to unload the gun, there'll be a short delay.

Peter reaches into the pocket of the unconscious Kit, and brings out a handful of cartridges. He places himself between Selena and the door and proceeds to load the gun, while talking to Selena

The smell of violets permeates the theatre

Selena Peter, I've had sufficient lunacy for one night. What the hell is going on?

Peter I'm sorry, but I realized last month that you had to go: when the bank threatened to foreclose on the mortgage.

Selena Am I hallucinating? Bank? Mortgage?

Peter I've worked damned hard to build up Crescent TV. And the only thing that can save it is your life insurance money. It's over two million, you know. You're a big star.

Selena I'm beginning to think you're serious.

Peter Entirely, I'm afraid. The problem was, if a wife is murdered, the husband is always the first suspect. Then I remembered that an ex-lover's usually the second suspect.

Selena My God! You mean, you set all this up!

Peter Rather cleverly for a state school boy, I think. "Paranormal" was the perfect way to put you alongside an ex-boyfriend. And a mentally suspect one, at that. I enjoyed winding him up, and faking his attempt to kill me. Two cuts with a penknife's a small price to pay.

Selena now knows she's in mortal danger. She decides to keep Peter talking, while looking furtively at the door and windows for an escape route

Selena So … Kit didn't shoot Terri?

Peter No, that was my mistake. I'd taken Camberston's gun from the rack, to await my chance. When I thought I saw you by the van, I fired. Then I came up to tell Joe and Terri Camberston had shot you. When I found you here, I had to adapt. (*He catches one of Selena's furtive glances*) Too late to run, Selena. The gun's loaded now. You wouldn't last two seconds.

Selena But … But you killed that young girl for nothing! And you show no remorse at all!

Peter I don't believe in remorse, I think it's a Jewish invention. I felt no remorse when I loosened the steering on Camberston's car and the wrong person died. I feel no remorse now.

Selena How could I live with you all these years, and not see you're a psychopath?

Peter Too busy with your career, my dear, and your perfect appearance. Anyway, it's all worked out rather well. Joe will have told the police that Camberston's a homicidal maniac, out to kill you. So when they find you both dead, and me hiding in the stables, they'll be happy to call it murder and suicide. Camberston's saved me a bit of effort by putting his finger prints on the gun.

Selena You're going to kill Kit as well?

Peter I think that's the kindest way. I can't believe a toff like him would enjoy ten years in jail for murder. Right, time's up.

Selena (*pleading*) Peter! For God's sake! Didn't you ever love me?

Peter Not really, no. I enjoyed taking you from Camberston. And it's been good having a glamorous wife to show off. But it's over now, Selena. It should have been over five minutes ago, if the gun had worked.

Selena Peter! Please!

Peter I'll make it easy for you. Turn your back, I'll be quick, you won't know a thing about it. If you don't co-operate, it could be messy and painful. So — turn your back, Selena.

Reluctantly, Selena turns her back. Peter moves up behind her and points the gun at the back of her head

Peter Funny — Renfield House will feature a clever husband with a dead wife and lover, just like before!

Suddenly, the Lights dim and the sound of the piano is heard, stunning the hearers with loud incisive chords. Peter freezes, and lowers the gun in bewilderment. Selena turns and both look at the piano in amazement. In the gloom, an area of the dust sheet before the piano seems to be rising up. It is above where a player would sit, and appears to be covering a human shape (See Note p. 48)

Peter and Selena stand transfixed while the piano completes its brief sequence of dramatic chords. Finally, Peter advances cautiously and snatches the dust sheet from the piano. He pulls it off to reveal nothing but the piano and an empty stool

During the following, Selena moves away and shelters behind some furniture; Kit recovers and gets to his feet

Peter My God! This room *is* haunted! Camberston's bloody ancestors are as crazy as he is! Well, nothing's changed, Selena. I'm afraid you still have to join them.

Peter raises the gun again. Kit grabs the gun barrel

Kit All right, Sims, I'll take that!
Peter Oh no, you won't, you bastard!

The two men wrestle for control of the gun, and their struggle takes them through the open balcony door, and out of sight along the balcony

After a few moments, a shot is heard

Selena watches the balcony door anxiously

Peter walks in, carrying the gun

Selena gasps

Peter raises the gun and aims at Selena. Briefly, we fear the worst: but then blood starts to spread over the front of Peter's sweater, his legs buckle and he falls to the ground

Kit enters, moves to Selena, and puts his arm round her

Kit Silly of him to hold the gun against his stomach. If he'd joined the Officer Training Corps, they'd have warned him about that. It's all right, darling, the nightmare's over.
Selena Thank you, Kit. Can we wait for the police downstairs?

They walk towards the door

Kit Yes. Come along, let's leave the ghosts behind.
Selena But they weren't all hostile, were they? I think Philomel just saved my life.

Kit and Selena exit, closing the door behind them

The CURTAIN *falls*

FURNITURE AND PROPERTY LIST

ACT I
Scene 1

On stage: Piano
Table
Chairs
Chaise-longue
Dust sheets
Small vase containing drooping flowers
Two Indian clubs
Boxes
Window curtains closed but slightly parted

Off stage: TV equipment. Minimum requirement: camera, lamp on stand, sound recording and playback equipment, cables and leads, screwdriver (**Peter, Terri** and **Joe**)

Personal: **Kit**: silver-knobbed stick (carried throughout Act I)
Peter: mobile phone in holder on belt
Terri: rucksack containing notepad and pen, torch
Selena: handbag containing mobile telephone and diary

Scene 2

Re-set: Tall stand lamp on floor

Off stage: Notebook (**Selena**)
Cables near ventilator opening (**Joe**)

During black-out p.23

Set: Blood on portrait of Philomel (or replace Philomel portrait with identical picture with blood on it) (**Stage Management**)

ACT II
SCENE 1

Re-set: Remove blood and gash from Philomel's portrait (or replace with original picture) (**Stage Management**)

Off stage: Torch (**Kit**)
Bottle of brandy and two glasses (**Joe**)

Personal: **Kit**: new walking-stick
Terri: large plaster

SCENE 2

Off stage: Shotgun (**Kit**)

Personal: **Peter**: knob from **Kit**'s first stick, thick cotton gloves, blood bag
Kit: handful of shotgun cartridges in pocket

LIGHTING PLOT

Practical fittings required: TV lamps
One interior with window backing. The same throughout

ACT I, SCENE 1

To open: Darkness in room; grey wintry light on window backing, dimming to black-out as scene progresses

Cue 1	**Kit** switches on the overhead light *Bring up general interior lighting*	(Page 1)
Cue 2	**Joe** looks around and sees the screwdriver *Overhead light flickers throughout following action*	(Page 12)
Cue 3	**Joe** continues towards the screwdriver *Black-out*	(Page 12)

ACT I, SCENE 2

To open: General interior lighting; darkness on window backing

Cue 4	**Selena** drops the phone *Lights flicker and fade during following action*	(Page 23)
Cue 5	Piano and sobbing sounds begin *Fade to black-out*	(Page 23)
Cue 6	When notified by **Stage Management** *Bring up TV spotlight on painting*	(Page 23)

ACT II, SCENE 1

To open: Darkness

Cue 7	**Kit** switches on overhead light *Bring up general interior lighting*	(Page 25)

ACT II, SCENE 2

To open: General interior lighting

Cue 8	**Peter**: " … just like before!" *Dim lights*	(Page 42)

EFFECTS PLOT

ACT I

Cue 1   When ready   (Page 1)
Soft piano music; fade in sound of woman sobbing;
fade music and sobbing and bring up fluttering
and soft thumping sound as of a trapped bird

Cue 2   Curtain falls   (Page 12)
Enormous crash

Cue 3   **Selena** looks in her diary   (Page 22)
Faint scent of violets; temperature falls on thermometer

Cue 4   **Selena** calls **Peter**'s name into the phone. Silence   (Page 23)
Ear-piercing screech from telephone

Cue 5   Lights flicker and fade   (Page 23)
Sound of window slamming shut

Cue 6   **Selena** tries to pull the door open   (Page 23)
Piano music and sobbing as Cue 1

Cue 7   **Selena** faints. A moment's silence   (Page 23)
Unearthly female scream

ACT II

Cue 8   **Terri**: "… and then perhaps you can rest."   (Page 28)
Piano plays

Cue 9   **Joe** looks up in horror   (Page 28)
Piano stops playing with crashing discord

Cue 10   **Joe** switches on the recording machine   (Page 34)
Recording of séance plays

Cue 11   **Joe** turns up the volume   (Page 35)
Bring up volume of séance recording

Cue 12   **Joe** adjusts a knob on the machine   (Page 35)
Increase bass and add sobbing sound

Cue 13   **Joe** makes another adjustment   (Page 35)
            Increase bass further

Cue 14   **Joe** switches off the machine   (Page 35)
            Cut séance recording

Cue 15   **Selena** peers intently at the machine. Silence   (Page 35)
            Gunshots

Cue 16   **Selena** spools the tape back to the start and activates it   (Page 39)
            Recording of séance plays quietly

Cue 17   **Selena** switches off the machine   (Page 39)
            Cut séance recording

Cue 18   **Peter** loads the shotgun   (Page 41)
            Smell of violets

Cue 19   Lights dim   (Page 42)
            Piano plays: loud, incisive chords

Cue 20   **Kit** and **Peter** move out of sight on the balcony   (Page 43)
            Gunshot

NOTES ON EFFECTS

The scent of violets. In the Sonning production, a violet scent was pumped into the theatre via the air-conditioning system. An alternative would be for a member of the Stage Management team to spray scent in the wings.

The ghostly outline effect. The effect in which Peter pulls off the dust-sheet and there is no-one there, proved impossible to achieve on the apron stage at Sonning. Instead, the removal of the sheet revealed an actress (Terri) portraying the ghost of Philomel. Directors are welcome to improvize: all that is required is a ghostly effect to divert Peter from firing his gun.

                                                        Edward Taylor

MANAGEMENT OF FIREARMS AND OTHER WEAPONS IN PRODUCTIONS

Recommended reading:

Entertainment Information Sheet No. 20 (Health and Safety Executive). This information sheet is one of a series produced in consultation with the Joint Advisory Committee for Broadcasting and the Performing Arts. It gives guidance on the management of weapons that are part of a production, including firearms, replicas and deactivated weapons. It is obtainable from: HSE Books, PO Box 1999, Sudbury, Suffolk, CO10 2WA. Tel: 01787 881165, Fax: 01787 313995. Or it may be downloaded from: www.hse.gov.uk

Home Office Firearms Law: Guidance to the Police. The Stationery Office 2002. ISBN 0 11 341273 8. Also available from: www.homeoffice.gov.uk

Health and Safety in Audio-visual Production: Your legal duties. Leaflet INDG360. HSE Books 2002

COPYRIGHT MUSIC

A licence issued by Samuel French Ltd to perform this play does not include permission to use the Incidental music specified in this copy. Where the place of performance is already licensed by the PERFORMING RIGHT SOCIETY a return of the music used must be made to them. If the place of performance is not so licensed then application should be made to the PERFORMING RIGHT SOCIETY, 29-33 Berners Street, London W1T 4AB.

A separate and additional licence from PHONOGRAPHIC PERFORMANCES LTD, Ganton House, 1 Upper James Street, London W1R 3HG is needed whenever commercial recordings are used.